INSPIRING WOMEN TODAY

---

3 TRUE STORIES, VOLUME A
EXCERPTS FROM
21 TRUE STORIES, VOLUME 1

INSPIRING WOMEN TODAY

3 TRUE STORIES, VOLUME A
EXCERPTS FROM
21 TRUE STORIES, VOLUME 1

Denise Duncan • Diane Diaz • Audrey Boland

WRITTEN AND COMPILED BY RODNEY MILES TABER

POWERS PRESS

Copyright © 2019 by Rodney Miles Taber
All rights reserved.
Published by Powers Press, an imprint of Bimini Books

No part of this book may be reproduced in any manner without written permission except in the case of brief quotations embodied in critical articles and reviews.

Although the author and publisher have made every effort to ensure that the information in this book was correct at press time, the author and publisher do not assume and hereby disclaim any liability to any party for any loss, damage, or disruption caused by errors or omissions, whether such errors or omissions result from negligence, accident, or any other cause. Forms and agreements are included for your information only.

For information about special discounts for bulk purchases or author interviews, appearances, and speaking engagements please contact:

Rodney Miles Taber
www.inspiringwomentoday.com
rmiles@inspiringwomentoday.com

Second Edition

ISBNS
Paperback/Perfect Bound: 978-1-946875-43-3
Hardcover/Case Laminate: 978-1-946875-44-0
Digital/Ebook: 978-1-946875-30-3

Written, compiled, cover, and book design by Rodney Miles:
www.RODNEYMILES.com
Cover image: 3Motional Studio / Pexels

in·spire

verb

1. fill (someone) with the urge or ability to do or feel something; create (a feeling, especially a positive one) in a person; animate someone with (such a feeling).

2. breathe in (air); inhale.

Origin: Middle English enspire, from Old French inspirer, from Latin inspirare 'breathe or blow into' from in- 'into' + spirare 'breathe'. The word was originally used of a divine or supernatural being, in the sense 'impart a truth or idea to someone.' —GOOGLE

Me and my wife Dawn in one of our favorite places, Gatlinburg, Tennessee

For Dawn

"I know of no greater happiness
than to be with you all the time,
without interruption,
without end."

—Franz Kafka

CONTENTS

INTRODUCTION ♦ 1

FALSE EVIDENCE APPEARING REAL ♦ 5
Denise Duncan

GOOD GRIEF ♦ 23
Diane Diaz

MEXICO ♦ 41
Audrey Boland

WANT MORE? ♦ 69

PHOTO CREDITS ♦ 70

(Left) Four more of my favorite women:
From left to right, Aunt Raye, Fallon (my daughter),
Mom (Ronna), and Nana (Jeannette)

INTRODUCTION

"Sure, he was great, but don't forget that Ginger Rogers did everything he did—backwards and in high heels."

—BOB THAVES, cartoonist

FOR WHATEVER REASON, I seem to have always enjoyed the company of and gravitated toward strong women. Even as a book collaborator over the last decade, my client list must be comprised 80 percent of women. So I wanted to celebrate women and once I had the basic framework for this project and announced it, the response was instant and energetic. And one of the things I enjoy most about a project like *Inspiring Women Today* is how as you conduct interviews common themes seem to bubble to the surface. They have for this, *Volume A*, as well as the larger *Volume 1. Paying it forward* is one of the themes, as you'll see. So is strength, both in small and large ways.

In these pages you'll find the joys, hopes, tragedies, triumphs, and wisdom each author has been brave and generous enough to share. My primary requirement for authors involved in this project has been candor, and the women involved really have been candid, often in such bold ways. I am truly grateful to each of them, because the hope is to create a series of books women of all ages and backgrounds can have whenever they need or might enjoy a dose of inspiration.

For example, I remember being nine years old, bouncing a kickball by our seven-story apartment building in New York (Staten Island) and hearing the ice cream man's chimes. I looked to our third-floor window and hesitated to call for my mom, because I knew money was tight. But on that day I didn't have to ask. The window opened and Mom leaned out, smiling under her red hair. My heart jumped at her *smile*. She waved. I put the ball down and waved back. She dropped a clear sandwich bag tied at the top, filled with change, and it landed in my hands with a crunch. There was bound to be enough for me and my little brother, Aaron, and I saw him already among the kids surrounding the ice cream van in the middle of Lincoln Avenue.

I ran over, thinking, *cherry Italian ice*, and wondered what life was like for my mom. I remembered the fights that led to the divorce five years earlier. They used to fight in the kitchen when they thought we were asleep, and I used to sneak down from my bunk bed and out of my bedroom to watch from the safety of the stairs. Money seemed to be the problem, at least one of them. And I remembered her letting me climb into her bed when I was little, where she'd confide in me like an adult—it made us *friends*.

My mother, Ronna, moved us to those apartments because my aunts and uncles and even my grandparents lived in the same buildings and they would watch us when she was at either of her two jobs. I remember her up early, off to the train that took her to the Staten Island Ferry, which took her to Lower Manhattan where she got on and off of a bus and then walked blocks and boarded an elevator that lifted her to the 35th floor of One World Trade Center. And I remember her not appearing at home again until late at night, after her second job waitressing at Beefsteak Charlie's, in the frilly shorts they wore.

I also remember walks through Rockefeller Center at Christmas, tons of gifts below the tree each year, homecooked meals, private school and soccer league, and even an occasional vacation, usually around some family gathering somewhere. It was an incredible childhood. It pleased or

INTRODUCTION BY RODNEY MILES TABER

worried me most of the time. And it was inspiring.

My mother would surprise me again when at sixteen I explained my girlfriend and I had "decided to make love" and she was now late with her period. There, on the sidewalk in Pompano Beach outside our rented townhome, Mom paused walking her dachshund, and got serious, but not mad. "Well," she said, "I can raise the baby as my own and when the time comes, we can let him or her in on things, so you two can still go to college." But the test came back negative and we all calmed down.

My mother had a special relationship with her grandmother, Hannah, who was very strong. As a young girl Hannah Sanger rode in a wagon out west to Nebraska where her parents claimed land—a homestead—where she watched them bake bread and play the accordion for the Native Americans that showed up. As a young woman herself, she ran the farm while her boys were fighting in World War II. When Hannah was older, in her nineties, my mother asked her, "Grandma, you did so much for us. How do we repay you?"

"You repay me by taking care of *your* children," she said.

My mother is still there for me, and my wife has a similar story with her mother, Sandy—single mom, two jobs, warm holidays, and still there for her. Without my own wife, Dawn, this book would not exist—Heck, *I might not exist!* Together for 30 years, she is an amazing wife, mother, and still my best friend. She made reinvention of myself at 40 (as a writer) possible. Before that, she sold rugs with me on the side of the road, laid tile, remodeled and flipped houses with me, then built a massage therapy practice, closing it when her hand-crafted "dragon wings" (for bearded dragons) business took off.

When we had our daughter, Fallon, she just seemed to know what to do. She is a perfect mother, and Fallon a pure blessing of a daughter. I watch Fallon rise early, go to work, study hard, and enjoy a beautiful relationship with a brilliant young man. I watch her laugh with her friends and truly care about others.

I'm humbled and grateful for the women in my life. I sincerely hope you find reading these books and connecting with these amazing women as inspiring as I found interviewing them. Women have power and magic—they are sacred, and that includes you.

Please enjoy *Inspiring Women Today*.

FALSE EVIDENCE APPEARING REAL

by Denise Duncan

> "I will love the light for it shows me the way, yet I will endure the darkness because it shows me the stars."
> —Og Mandino

IT'S BEEN QUITE a bumpy little ride, life in general. For lack of a better term, and with complete self-respect, I am one, *tough old broad*. (That could be the name of a book! I love it.) Some of the best times of my life were in my early childhood. I was the baby of the family, with one brother and two sisters. We were all born and raised in Southern California and our parents provided us with a fun-loving and stable family home. Life was wonderful until I turned 13 years of age, when—let's just play nice and say I was a "spirited" teenager. And oh, the hell I put my mom and dad through—the whole family, really. I still have deep regrets but I've learned if you don't forgive yourself, you can never truly heal or grow. But by the ripe, old age of 17 I was a full-blown drug addict. By 19 my parents admitted me to a psychiatric hospital, a drug rehab. And these were some of the darkest times of my life.

This "rehab" managed to get me off of street drugs but replaced them with psych drugs. After several months of this drug treatment, a couple of surgeries, and a medical drug catastrophe, I ended up in a deep psychotic state for an extended period of time. The scariest part of it all was when I didn't even recognize my own parents. *Oh man, was I ever in for the fight of my life!* My dear sister Cindy was the only one I could really recognize, so she put her own life on hold, stayed with me at the psych hospital, and helped to put her baby sister back together again. My love and gratitude for my family is immeasurable.

A couple of years after getting clean and working on myself to become an acceptable part of the human race and my family again, I met a wonderful guy with dreams of marrying him someday. He was in the Air Force and quite the catch for a girl with my past. Well, instead of this being the perfect fairytale I had hoped for, I ended up getting pregnant and he decided to leave. Despite that, having my daughter Amanda was the best decision I have ever made. She saved my life. It was never easy being a single mom, but oh my gosh, is she ever worth it! It's hard to believe she's already 32 years old. What an incredible woman she has grown to be. Without question, She is my greatest source of true love and pride.

Denise and daughter Amanda

Had I not been a drug addict at a very young age and gone through some of the things I've gone through, my dream would have been to go to college and be a newscaster, a journalist. Instead, I took the rough road, and believe it or not, I'm glad I did.

FALSE EVIDENCE APPEARING REAL BY DENISE DUNCAN

IN 1997 I FOUND myself doing payroll for 800 employees for a huge, huge water transmission pipe company. I used to drop my daughter Amanda off each morning with my parents at their house and I'd go to work. Amanda would have breakfast there and they'd drive her to school (she had a lunch card I had to budget for). My mom would pick her up after school and care for her until I got off of work. Mom would cook them all dinner and save a plate for me, which I would eat each night when I picked Amanda up. That was usually my only meal of the day. I was working twelve hours a day with no overtime since I was paid a salary—a small salary with benefits, so I could at least take care of my daughter. My parents were of the belief that if they gave me too much I would just take more, and I agree with that 100 percent. They charged me childcare and a portion for the food, and well they should have. It wasn't a large amount but enough to learn from—in fact, that's part of my tenacity to keep going. It never was a handout, and they were always there to help me when I needed them.

Soon after, my parents retired and decided to sell Watkins[1], sometimes at state and county fairs. While at the L.A. County Fair, they saw a live Kitchen Craft[2] cooking demonstration, and they met two of the company's top salespeople (David and Rebecca Monge). They told my sister Julie about it, and soon after she and her husband Alan signed up to sell Kitchen Craft cookware and started training. What did they have to lose? They had four kids to raise and they needed to make more money. After they were in it for a year, they were insanely successful and went on their first incentive trip to the Bahamas.

When they got back, they said to me, "You know, DD (my whole family calls me DD), you would really be good at this." I was grossly underpaid at the pipe company and had my daughter to raise, so what did I have to lose? — other than the fact that I would have to pay all of my own travel expenses, it was a commission-only sales job, and I didn't know the first thing about sales! I decided to go for it anyway, with financial help from my family to get started. I was going to

---

[1] Watkins Incorporated is a manufacturer of health remedies, baking products, and other household items. An independent sales force sells the products using various methods, including the Internet, person to person, trade shows, party planning, and fund-raising. The company was founded by J. R. Watkins in Plainview, Minnesota, who began selling liniment in 1868 door-to-door in the southeastern part of the state. By the 1940s, Watkins was the largest direct-sales company in the world, but soon began to decline. —Adapted from Wikipedia

[2] Read the fascinating story of Kitchen Craft here: https://kitchencraftcookware.com/ourstory/

reach for the stars, make my family proud, and make a better life for my daughter and myself.

Denise performing a cooking demonstration

When I left my job at the pipe company, the only pair of shoes I had were a pair of steel-toed boots issued to me by my employer. (If you've met me, if you've seen me, that's not my style!) When I showed up for training in those steel-toed boots, my sister was like, "What are you wearing?"

"Well," I said, "it's the only pair of shoes I've got." Those were the shoes I trained in and lived with right up until I got a schedule to go out on my own and make it to the "big leagues."

My daughter Amanda and I were living in Southern California, in the high desert, in Apple Valley. My daughter was 12 or 13 and in seventh grade at the time. I guess I didn't realize what a horrible thing it would be for her, taking her out of school at that point, away from her home and friends. But I didn't decide to do this to live the lifestyles of the rich and famous, I did it so I could provide for *both* of us. I always saw to it that Amanda was provided for. I, however, was usually not, with the little income I had. So that first summer after training I told her, "You're going with." She wasn't happy. She wanted to spend the summer with her friends. "This is going to make our lives better," I said, "and eventually you're going to understand why we have to do this."

My sister loaned me a Ford Aerostar minivan. Kitchen Craft loaned me a cargo trailer (that was pretty beat up) because we needed the van to be our house for a while. I loaded the cargo trailer to the brim with my booth and supplies. Now, I had never hooked up or pulled a cargo trailer before—no big deal, right? I was riddled with *fear*. I put a twin mattress in the van, my mom sewed us curtains for the windows, and we hit the road.

I was given a first-year-rookie schedule, where I wasn't making any money. We were up in Yreka, California at the Red Acres Fair, and I was flat broke. I didn't have gas or food, or anything—I didn't even have food for the demonstrations. We were staying in a KOA campground, and I knew there wasn't money in the bank, so I wrote them a hot check. Now, the show prior to that, there was money coming in, but they used to FedEx our checks to our home addresses. A friend of mine up in Apple Valley was supposed to pick up my check and put it in the bank, but she didn't. It wasn't a big check, it wouldn't even have covered the overdraft fees in my checking account at that point, that's how bad it was. We hadn't eaten in two days and my daughter finally said to me, "Mom, I'm just *hungry*."

"Okay," I said.

My parents were full-time RVers, so I couldn't call them collect to ask for help, because all they had was a cell phone and I didn't have one (they were still expensive and uncommon, and mine had been turned off). We got in the van, so low on gas it was running on fumes, and I drove us to a 7-11. I walked in and looked at the gentleman behind the counter and told him, "Hi. My name is Denise—Denise Duncan, if you need to know all that. I'm going to walk over there and I'm going to take one pack of powdered donuts and one jug of chocolate milk for my daughter. We haven't eaten and I don't have any money, so I'm stealing them, and you have two options: You can turn a blind eye, or you can call the police, but that's what I'm doing. I'm really sorry, but I just have to do this." I went over and took them, and as I walked out, he winked and turned his back to me.

When I got in the van, Amanda said, "Mom! You just make everything better somehow! I don't know how you do it, but these aren't just for me, they're for us."

I looked at her and I said, "Honey, every one of those six donuts is yours. They've got your name all over them. Your momma's gonna be just fine."

We went to the local police station since I had no way of calling anyone for help. I went in an explained my circumstances, and the lovely gal at the desk phoned my parents for me. My dear dad once again came to my rescue and sent me enough money via Western Union for food and gas to get home. I was too tired to drive through the night, though, so we slept in a truck stop. Actually, my daughter slept in a truck stop that night. My eyes were wide open, because I was *petrified*.

After that, most people would have never, ever gone on to another show again. I had promised my daughter, "We're going to have a great time," and this was the outcome, right? No.

Lights / Denise Duncan

I believed in myself—and I think that's what I would want every woman to hear, louder than anything. It's nice to have a family that cares and is there to hold you up, and it's nice to have a significant other to hold you up and be a team, but for me, there is an "I" in "team." So, instead of giving up, I marched on. I went from taking my daughter away from home in the middle of summer to stealing food at a 7-11 and sleeping in a van at a truck stop to *success* I had just never imagined.

I was doing live demonstrations for the oldest, largest, stainless steel cookware manufacturer in the world. I did lengthy demonstrations that turned strangers into family in two hours and gave them the catapult to good health. That's what I did for a living. That's how I felt about it and I still do. I traveled all over the United States. I would be gone sometimes a couple of months at a time from my daughter who was at a tender and very impressionable age. But I made a decision to do it for us both.

If my story seems strong, emotional, and maybe even hard to hear, the story of my mentor and dear friend Dave Hurley (owner of Kitchen Craft) is eight thousand times more difficult than mine. I saw such *conviction* in him and I believed it. I learned from him that you can overcome any and all of what life throws at you, as long as believe in yourself. If he could do it, well then, so could I.

Fear, to me, was being a single mom and not being able to pay the bills, not being able to keep a roof over our heads and keep Amanda fed. My daughter was a teenager and she believed she had to have that Roxy sweatshirt and designer tennis shoes to feel like she fit in. So, I made sure she had what she needed, and I made sure I provided for her, but at what cost to myself, right? But hey, I decided to have a child, and her dad decided to leave, so this is what we're going to do. Kitchen Craft taught me how to manage that. I learned I was always my own worst enemy in my head, always trying to "fix it," instead of just "doing it," and my favorite saying was (and is) "Clean out between your ears, girl! Otherwise, you will bring yourself down."

It was life changing when I started with Kitchen Craft and I went into a setting where I got this undying respect from complete strangers. When complete strangers treat you better than most people you call "friends," you find yourself learning more and more about yourself, and really, finding your own worth. Once I found my own worth, there was no holding me back. I was like, *Oh, my gosh, I'm so much more than I ever thought I was.* I had just never seen myself as being worth much.

That all changed when I could see what my peers saw in me and see the results of believing in myself as much as they did. It was the whole experience, the training (which was really more about life skills than selling cookware), and the sense of becoming a part of something that would make a difference in people's lives, as well as mine. And for the first time in my adult life, I finally felt like I was really good at something, and it made me feel valued! Truthfully, I'm the worst salesperson on the planet. I would *give it away* to everybody, but I was selling *hope*. It's the relatability and the love for people that I enjoy. And when you get to go back to those same venues year after year and your customers come and see you, they love on you like family.

Let's not forget this didn't happen overnight. The first five years of this kind of industry are going to make you or break you, and they break *everybody* long before we make it. It's true. But if you can just have the mindset that what you're doing is the right thing for you as a person, and that you can find a balance of self-joy in that, it will happen. Something happens where you get this innate ability to relate with people and for me that was my gratification, how much I enjoyed those people and how much those people enjoyed me. I knew I was in the right place. I had found my passion. It wasn't actually about massive monetary gain to me, which was probably my biggest self-employment failure. I was like, "Easy come, easy go." Success was never about having copious amounts of money. It's been about balance, and for me, about achievement, self-worth, and recognition. And I started to rise in the company.

I'll never forget my fifth year in the business. I was the keynote speaker at one of the conventions, and I was talking about the fear of being on the road by myself, and the fear of being away from my daughter and leaving her with my sister or her best friend's family—the fear of all of that, the *guilt* of all of that, even while I knew I was doing this for the betterment of my daughter, to be able to provide for her and our future. It's really a convoluted emotional thing to do, you know, stepping up and out of the box, stepping up and out of the comfort zone. And I was up there speaking when it all of a sudden hit me, and you could have heard a pin drop—

"Fear," I said, and I spelled it out: "F-E-A-R, fear, is nothing more than *false evidence appearing real*," which most of us have heard a million times by now, but at the time, I had never heard it. Yet it was what came out of my mouth. It wasn't in my little notes I was speaking from, but I said it, and I still remember what I felt:

Oh, watch out world, I'm coming for you! And once I figured out my *fears* were holding me back, I believed deeply I could achieve anything my heart desired!

The sincere recognition from this company was always a big part of what kept me going. That's just part of who I am. It really was for me, like, *Oh my gosh! I'm accomplishing things in my life!* When I earned my first Million Dollar Club trip (I had earned the annual incentive trips every year, but this was the first Million Dollar Club trip) there were only twelve of us who achieved that prestigious award that year.

We all went to New York for two days prior to embarking on—*oh my gosh*—the Queen Mary II. Remember my steel-toed boots? Well, we got to New York, we embarked on the Queen Mary II, and of course, this is all about the shoes I was embarking in. I had to look the part of the Queen Mary II. I had a red-and-white, polka-dotted scarf, blue pedal-pushers, a crisp white blouse and a pair of red wedge pumps like they used to wear in the '40s, with the little matching handbag. And I realized, *I was able to do that*? I had a 400-dollar *pair of shoes* to get on that ship in!—What?

Ferry and Fjords of Norway / Denise Duncan

Wow! I had arrived, and for a brief moment my shoes defined success for me. It didn't take me long to realize shoes really have very little to do with success or self-worth. (But I still adore those shiny little red shoes!)

We were on the Queen Mary II for seven days. We went to the QM2 island and got to hang out there for a day, but the trip was really all about enjoying the world's largest transatlantic ocean-liner across the great Atlantic Ocean. Things are different on a ship with the magnitude and prestige of the Queen Mary II. It's very, very old money and extremely wealthy people with a ballroom instead of a disco. (They did have a little disco on the back of the ship for the lower-class passengers, like me, Dave Hurley, and our cookware family.) Remember Rose and Jack from the movie, *Titanic*? Just sayin! [Laughter]

We all had a blast dancing the night away in that disco! Our days were spent relaxing and going to the spa, eating exquisite food, and enjoying the beauty of this magnificent ship! It was one of the best experiences of my life. And if that wasn't enough for a girl who was a single mom, who had been was sleeping in a van, who had been through the emotional warfare, drug addiction, and financial struggles I had been through, I was now in the Million-Dollar Club—the Diamond Club. I got a diamond ring, a leather jacket, and all of that recognition.

Wow, Just wow!

Once we got back to New York and disembarked from the QM2, our group of twelve got on a first-class flight to Boston for the second phase of our Million Dollar Club adventure. We stayed in beautiful suites at the world-famous Omni Parker House for three days. We toured the entire city and all of its history! Boston quickly became my favorite city in the U.S.! It was then time to meet up with the rest of our Kitchen Craft family for the "regular," annual incentive trip. They all flew into Boston and met up with the twelve of us as we hopped on a plane and flew to *Ireland*. All of this was *one trip*, we were gone for like three weeks.

When we landed in Shannon, Ireland, we got on a luxury, chartered bus and headed to our destination in Killarney. This was like my fifth incentive trip, maybe sixth. My first one was all over Europe—Italy, France, Spain, cruising the Mediterranean. But this was now the Million Dollar Club—nothing anybody with my background would have ever dreamed about. I would have never allowed myself to dream about stuff like this because it just wasn't attainable. We're told, "You've got to keep it real with yourself, remember that," or "Never set expectations too high, you'll just have disappointments." Remember that one? I would have never said, "I'm going on the Queen Mary II, then going to Boston, and finishing off the trip with a week in Ireland!"

Come on!

While we were in route to Killarney on the day of our arrival, we stopped at a real-life castle. There we had an authentic Irish breakfast. The castle was built in the 1600s. It was magical and amazing. We had porridge there—porridge! We all started singing the tune from the movie *Oliver*. And I'm thinking to myself, *Is this really happening, right now, in my life?* That night, all of us were so dog-tired after the long flight and everything we did that day, we checked into the hotel in Killarney and everyone was like, "Oh, please just let us sleep," as we did face-plants into our beds. *Ah, finally some rest!*

Not 15 minutes later the phone rang. It was Dave Hurley, our fearless leader! "Oh my gosh," he said, "did you know Michael Flatley's last Riverdance performance is tonight? Did you know tonight is the grand finale, right here in Killarney? I just bought us all tickets. You have one hour to meet up in the lobby." We jumped up, splashed cold water on our faces, and off we went! What an amazing experience that Riverdance was. It spoke to my soul and resides in my heart still today!

And our adventure was just getting started. Ireland is breathtakingly beautiful, and I was just about to experience it all! We saw the Gap of Dunloe[3], we did the Ring of Kerry[4], we kissed the Blarney Stone[5], we did all these things. We even spent our last night in Ireland at the world-class Adare Manor, where we had the entire 17th-century castle to ourselves for the night! What an insanely, magical, life-changing trip. I was pretty sure I was living a fairytale, and I was the one

---

[3] The Gap of Dunloe, also recorded as Bearna an Choimín, is a narrow mountain pass running north-south in County Kerry, Ireland, that separates the MacGillycuddy's Reeks mountain range in the west, from the Purple Mountain Group range in the east. —Wikipedia

[4] The Ring of Kerry (Irish: Mórchuaird Chiarraí) is a 179-kilometre-long (111-mile) circular tourist route in County Kerry, south-western Ireland. —Wikipedia

[5] The Blarney Stone (Irish: Cloch na Blarnan) is a block of Carboniferous limestone[1] built into the battlements of Blarney Castle, Blarney, about 8 kilometres (5 miles) from Cork, Ireland. According to legend, kissing the stone endows the kisser with the gift of the gab (great eloquence or skill at flattery). The stone was set into a tower of the castle in 1446. The castle is a popular tourist site in Ireland, attracting visitors from all over the world to kiss the stone and tour the castle and its gardens. —Wikipedia

who earned it! All because I conquered my *fear* and believed in myself!

Can you imagine, that was just one of many trips? What about the trip on the four-masted schooner through the Greek Isles? Oh, and cruising the fjords of Norway, just to name a few.

Did the trips give me the motivation to go out there and sell, sell, sell? Well, they certainly didn't hurt, but the trips were never really about motivation to me. They were about *recognition*. My motivation was what the cookware *does for people*—it always was.

But the money didn't hurt, either!

WE ALL HAVE expectations of what we are "supposed" to be doing, isn't that right? We have things that are "expected" or "required" of us. But if you just step outside of that box, the outcome is really quite amazing. After you make a million in sales, you have to continue to make a million in sales. You quickly learn the highs and lows of the direct sales industry. Outcomes are often not what you'd like to have happen, but that's just the nature of the business.

When the economy crashed in 2008, the cookware industry was hit hard. And by 2009, I was one of the many that lost everything. It took me a few years to get back on my feet, but I never quit or gave up, and for the *next* five years the cookware industry flourished! In looking back, I realized I had a false sense of security and should have been a better steward of my money (*whoa, what a defining moment!*). By late 2014, I was seeing an all too familiar trend in the business, and I knew the road ahead was going to be a really rough one. So, after a 15+ year career with Kitchen Craft, I decided it was time for new endeavors. It was the hardest business decision I've ever had to make. It was like losing a piece of myself. I miss it, that part of my life. Mostly, I miss my cookware family (my customers) but the business and the income just weren't what they once were, and I couldn't hold on any longer.

Soon after, my husband and I separated and he filed for divorce. It was at that point in my life I thought, *I'm not going to experience that again. I have experienced that collapse several times in my adult life and this time I am just not going to allow it to happen again.*

After my marriage of seven years fell apart, I found myself questioning my own self-worth. I was losing myself and feeling broken all over again. The craziest part about our marriage is that it wasn't conventional. I mean, we essentially lived and worked in separate states, owned

Beautiful Copenhagen, Denmark! | Denise Duncan

separate properties, and had separate bank accounts, which apparently didn't help us, because the demise of our marriage was all financial anyway. I watched the man I loved turn into someone I didn't even know. Oh man, did he get fierce once my money dried up and I was having to start a new business. But no matter what, it takes two to tango and we couldn't even agree to disagree! It was all just crazy and horrible!

Our divorce was finalized on February 16th 2018. I'm so relieved to be closing that chapter in my life. Life is way too short to spend it destroying each other. I've always been one to pull myself up by the boot straps, and keep marching on, but this divorce, it's been a toughie on me, that's for sure. I've decided to not let it define me, not now, not after all the hurdles I've overcome.

Today, I'm working on getting to know myself again, cleaning out between my ears, and constantly reminding myself to be proud of my life. I'm self-employed and I still love what I do for a living. I'm doing well financially. I'm healthy. I feel good. I'm even starting to date, (Oh my gosh, can you imagine, after like 15 years? *Whoa, how does this work now*? It's just awful!) But it sure does feel good to have a pulse again!

Life is always bound to change. Most women I know—myself included—don't like change. But if you learn to embrace it, change can be just what you need. So, I kicked myself into self-preservation mode, and decided it was time to downsize and get rid of my big, four-bedroom house. It was time to **let go** of all that stuff and start living a simpler life.

Denise Rapids | Kitchen Craft

I now live in Mesa, Arizona, in snowbird country, well known for its five-star RV/park model resorts with endless amenities. I now own a

400-square foot park model (like a "tiny" house) that I got for next-to-no money in one of these cool resorts. I had it completely remodeled, put my style and pizzazz into it, and turned it into my own little Nantucket cottage. Cutest thing you've ever seen, and I'm mortgage free! Think that took some of the pressure off? You bet it did! It's exactly where I was meant to land.

I didn't go belly-up. I minimized. I bought myself a smaller new car and a nice little work van. I started my own business ten minutes from home, at the Mesa Marketplace. I have my very own storefront along with 1,500 other vendors selling their goods. I've been there for three and a half years now, selling a variety of products, including a healthy ceramic cookware—cookware is my *passion*, and I'm really good at it.

I refer to the "light at the end of the tunnel" all the time. My parents, my daughter, my dear friends are always like, "Man, that Denise? She just takes a licking and keeps on ticking. And when she walks in the room, she has a glorious smile—*But how? Why?*" I think my strongest quality is that I have never given up, that no matter how bad it gets, or how deep I have to dig, I refuse to stay there. I'm a true believer in the greater good. Period.

August 4th of this year will be my 35th anniversary of being clean. That's pretty heavy, huh? I very proudly call that my greatest achievement. And as far as what keeps me going, first is my faith. Second, my obligation as a parent to be present and mentally healthy for my only child, Amanda. Lastly, my dear parents. I need to be strong for them, and not let them down. They've been through enough. I want to be there for them, as they have always been there for me.

And I know my worth, I believe in myself. And whether you **believe** you can or you can't, **you'd be right, either way.**

About Denise Duncan

Denise is available as a keynote speaker!

To find out more and make arrangements, visit

www.INSPIRINGWOMENTODAY.com

Gap of Dunloe (Ireland)

Daniel Dudek

GOOD GRIEF

by Diane Diaz

"Although the world is full of suffering, it is full also of the overcoming of it."

—Hellen Keller

I AM NO STRANGER to grief. I was four years old when I saw my first deceased person. She used to work in the household of my maternal grandparents, and I remember going down to the church with my mom. It wasn't a scary moment for me, though. In fact, I had an inner knowing that it was a sacred moment and a very special occasion. Now, I'm what most people recognize as a rainbow baby[6]. I grew up understanding I had a sibling who died as a baby whom I never met. And since the age of four I have

---

[6] A rainbow baby "is a baby born after a miscarriage, stillborn, or neonatal death," Jennifer Kulp-Makarov, M.D., FACOG, explained to Parents.com. "It is called a

experienced major losses about every two years up until the age of 33, whether it was death by illness, death by homicide, accidental death, traumatic death, infantile death—you name it, I was exposed to it. In my culture it was very acceptable to have funeral rituals and to participate with the elderly and neighbors who were sick, so it was something that was very normal and natural to me and I always gravitated toward those who were hurting.

A lot of people don't talk about grief, or they think grief is only death, dying, and bereavement. That brings about a lot of *death anxiety.* My passion, my mission in life, is to bring about support for the grieving, and to empower ourselves to *companion* grief instead of avoiding it or participating in myths that we have been long conditioned into believing about grief. *Compassion* is one of the greatest gifts that we can give each other, and compassion is something that can be learned. Sympathy, empathy, and compassion are not the same things, and a lot of people have a misconception about them. But it doesn't have to be that way.

I WAS BORN in 1970 in New Jersey, a natural-born American citizen of Puerto Rican descent, and I was raised in South Florida, coming here at the age of seven or eight years old. In high school my whole idea was to join the military, but I got pregnant, and at that time they had just passed a law saying you could not join the military if you had dependents.

---

rainbow baby because it is like a rainbow after a storm: something beautiful after something scary and dark." She adds, "It is an extremely emotional and devastating experience to lose a pregnancy [or baby]. To create a life or bring a baby into the world after such a loss is amazing like a miracle for these parents."
—https://www.parents.com/baby/what-it-means-to-be-a-rainbow-baby-and-why-rainbow-babies-are-beautiful/

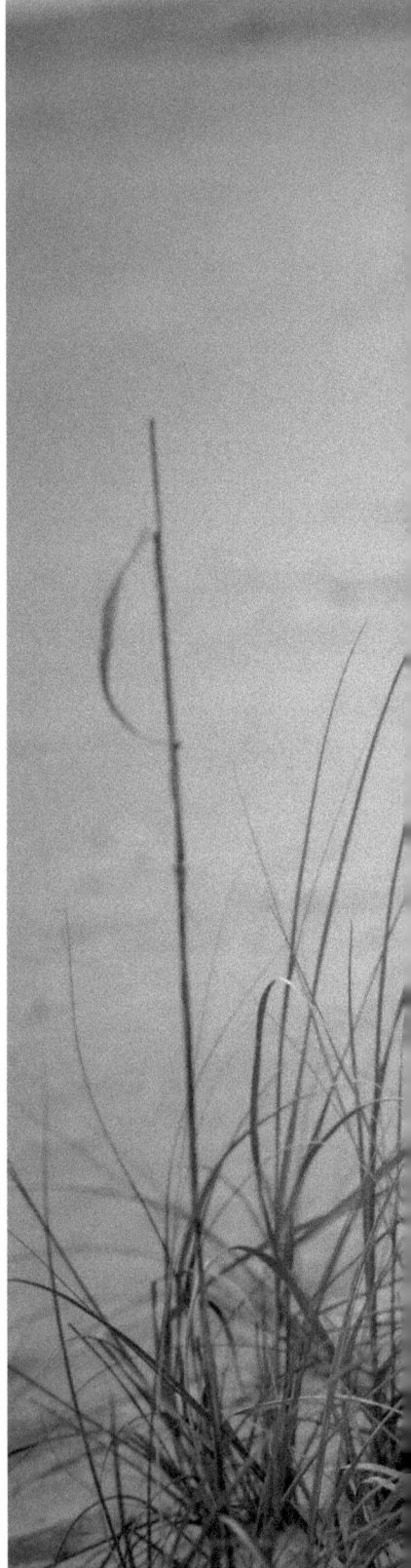

Because I was in the delayed enlistment program, I had to drop out, and that was a whole different type of grieving in itself. I had to come to terms all of a sudden with the fact that I would not live my dream of becoming an officer, and I had to reinvent myself.

I got married, my husband joined the military, and we left South Florida. (My first career was in accounting because that's what I was good at and that's what I studied in school. My certificate in financial studies served me well for my first twenty years.) We started our military career in Spain. We were young with two babies and poor, but it was amazing! The best place to live and be poor is in Europe. It was nice to be able to just jump in a car and do staycations anywhere you wanted to. We were stationed overseas for ten years.

In 1999, my father-in-law died, and we were getting ready to move back to the United States. After we did, my son Sergio was diagnosed with cancer just a month before his 9th birthday, when he was eight years old. At this critical time for me, I remember Oprah had a series on her TV show called *Honoring the Spirit*. It empowered me and gave me permission to do self-care, to not have to be everything for everyone all the time, because that was running me ragged and leaving me resentful. And I think that was the beginning for me of recognizing there was more to life than the constant hustle and bustle and just trying to survive. Being an A-type personality, I was very controlling and very perfectionistic, and she, Oprah, helped me relinquish some of that. So, I have to give a shout out to my girl, Oprah. It was the beginning of a transformation for me and I often tell people that I went from analyzing numbers to analyzing behaviors, to analyzing grief.

Parents don't want to bury their children. If your parents die, you become an orphan. If your spouse dies, you're a widow or a widower. But if your child dies, it's so taboo that there is no culture on Earth that has a name or a label for that. In that, there is a certain isolation and a certain stigma because people are very uncomfortable talking about a deceased child. No one wants to plan a funeral, no one wants to talk about a child dying, because that brings up the reality of their own children's mortality, or their own grandchildren's mortality. And in that I found I was able to provide my years of knowledge, my years of companioning, which I did normally and naturally to help people.

Even before I went into my current career full-time, I was an 11th Hour Volunteer[7]. When somebody is actively dying. I would provide respite care for family members so that as their loved one was dying, they could go to the bathroom or down to the cafeteria at the hospital and not worry that their loved one would die by themselves. Or, sometimes those passing didn't even have family and were just kind of alone, so I'd stay with them.

But it wasn't until my own son was diagnosed with cancer, relapsed from cancer, and died from cancer that I realized my calling was (and always had been) in grief, in bereavement, in supporting other people. As I was trying to get that support, I found there were a lot of professionals—doctors, even psychologists—who didn't know how to appropriately support me or my family while we were grieving because they were so uncomfortable with their own ideas and their own hang-ups.

After a two-and-a-half-year battle with cancer, Sergio died on April 4, 2002. He was 11 years old. To get through the loss, I became very aware of what was going on for me. I knew it was okay for me to feel the way I was feeling and that I didn't have to follow what other people said or expected of me about going through grief. I think that came from watching others grieving with people invalidating or trying to stifle their grief, and I knew there had to be a better way.

I became very comfortable with silence and stillness and I will often say that while my faith wasn't broken, it was shaken, and it was a time in my life of a lot of soul-searching, a lot of searching for meaning, a lot of understanding that I wasn't alone even though I felt very, very alone. Part of getting through that was honoring myself, respecting the process, and being willing to take a step back.

I realized there was a really big need to support people. There are times when becoming an expert in your own grief is what ends up being the healing and the "out" of living with that consistently. So, I went back to school in 2002. I took a sabbatical because we moved to the Florida panhandle, then we adopted two girls (a sibling group), so my focus changed for a little bit, but I eventually got a bachelor's degree in social psychology in 2011.

Today, I teach a lot of *mindful* grieving. After you've had a significant loss, you are usually

---

[7] https://www.gohospice.com/11th-hour-volunteering-keeping-vigil-patients-bedside/

either constantly doing busy work, in a sense avoiding the reality of what's going on (though you can't really avoid it), or you're stuck, staying in that consistent cycle of living the death story. I could have focused on how my son died and what led up to his death, but I chose to focus on his life, and not just making it about his death. I do believe with Sergio's care there were some mistakes made, but the empathic part of me knows that I did the best I could with what I had and those around me did the best they could with what they had. Was it perfect? Absolutely not. But being able to be open to that process really helped a lot of the healing. It's going on 17 years in April and there's still a lot of healing work for me. New grief will often bring up pieces of old grief.

After Sergio died, I was perfectly okay with the thought of not having more children, so I thought. I think one of the things that happens when you get tossed into a significant loss like death or the loss of a big relationship, you end up indifferent to having that thing happen again, you lose that sense of death anxiety. I no longer had death anxiety. It was just like, *Okay, I've seen death, I've witnessed death, I've held death in my hands, and if it comes, it comes.*

Diane and daughter | Estelle Zaret | EZ Photography

Part of me did want more children and the other part of me was okay if I didn't. So, when we looked at adopting the girls it was just one of those moments of synchronicity. Things aligned. My oldest biological daughter was 16 at the time. We started taking the adoption classes, and my (adopted) girls were wards of the state so they were in the foster care system. That kind of checked that box off for me, where I wasn't starting off new at 35, but at the same time, Dave and I were at the end of his military career, so we had built the home, we had a stable relationship, we were at that point in our lives where we could offer more. And why not? We had the means, we had the desire, and we decided to go ahead and adopt these girls.

Sergio taught me a lot in his first eleven years of life. If you're a parent I'm sure that by watching your child grow up, you have evolved, and you're probably a proud parent at that, just as I am about my kiddos. They teach us so much, not just about how they see the world, but how we see the world and how we end up adapting to it. So, Sergio taught me a lot about his life, but in his death, I learned so much more.

I would not have done this, I would not be the person I am without his dying. For me it was, *Okay, there's a reason for this, there's a reason for everything that happens.* And for others, they were like, "What possible reason could there be for a child to waste away for two and a half years and die from cancer? What possible reason could there be for God to need another soul up in Heaven?" It goes back to what we find meaning in, and I choose that I don't want my son's life to be in vain, and I sure as hell don't want his death to be in vain.

In his legacy, in honoring his life, in celebrating his life, I am taking those lessons and I am passing them on so that maybe somebody doesn't have to go through the pain or the burden exactly the way I did. Maybe a little bit of what I share is enough—even if it's for a moment—to give someone a sense of relief. And that's enough for me.

SOUTH FLORIDA—Coral Springs, Coconut Creek, Broward County—was my stomping ground growing up and I still go back and visit there frequently. Three weeks ago, I was down in the Parkland area because we were doing the communal trauma support training for the Parkland shooting[8]. We have that anniversary coming up, on the 14th of February.

When we are impacted by grief, we don't have a choice but to continue living life *changed.* Not that we want to, we're just kind of thrown into it and it's either sink or swim, it's do the best that you can. There are people who think they can stuff grief away but when they least expect it, it comes back up. One of my tag lines is "meaningful living despite everyday grieving." While we never fully get over grief, I believe we

---

[8] On February 14, 2018, a gunman opened fire at Marjory Stoneman Douglas High School in Parkland, Florida, killing seventeen students and staff members and injuring seventeen others. —Wikipedia

can grow from it. Does everybody? No. You have to be open to it because experiencing grief is vulnerable. Society tells us we have to be successful at everything we do, and that failure is not okay. Right?

But who gets to decide, who gets to define that? Well, *how do we learn if we don't fail?* If we don't fail and we don't analyze what went wrong, how can we grow from that? Grief is the same way. People don't want to lean into all that messy stuff because they're afraid they're going to get stuck in it, going to get judged by it, and like they're opening Pandora's Box.

And there's that misconception that you can't control it. Sometimes controlling and compartmentalizing, especially for our A-type personality people, serves you well in grief. You learn how to use those skills you already have for what it is that you need, and I'm of the belief that we all possess those skills innately. It's just that when we're in a crisis, when we're scared, when we're worried, when we are angry, we lose sight of that because our brains are naturally designed to help us survive. You often hear people say when they're angry, "I see blood! I see red!" When you go into that red zone, your brain is no longer making those connections to help you think

Monsters / Estelle Zaret / EZ Photography

clearly. When you're in deep grief, you're in a life crisis, you're in an existential crisis.

So, what do you do? It depends on the person. There has to be a lot of validating. There has to be normalizing. Everything we think is abnormal becomes normal in grief. People don't want to hear that. People often say to me, "I feel like I'm going crazy, like I'm spinning out of control, like this tape recorder in my head (whether it's a voice, an image, a thought) doesn't want to stop." That's because our brains are wired to problem-solve. It's like a computer, it's going to try different things to fill in the blank. And when you feed it information, it no longer has to fill in the blank by itself.

When we learn about our nature like this and we learn a few techniques it can make big differences for us as well as those around us. I teach people who want to compassionately connect that the first thing is to remain present: "I'm really pissed off right now because this guys was being lewd with my wife. What did that mean to me?" Was it that you felt inadequate in being able to protect her or in being able to stop or control that situation? Was it that you were disrespected? Was it that this person had no respect for a married woman or a *woman,* for that matter?

We have those people too, who don't care, it's just all about them and what they want or what they're fantasizing about in that moment. So, it's about remaining present: "What's going on for me, right now?" Usually what's happening is that you have some kind of core belief, some value, some moral that has just been offended at such a deep level that you get that reaction. When you back up from it you can start to be rational again, but sometimes it takes a while for the brain to calm down.

There's this tiny little piece within our brain, the amygdala[9], the reptilian part of the brain, where the fight, flight, or freeze responses come from. Our brains are designed to respond initially and automatically from that place, and when that piece of the brain is stuck, it's kind of like when you put your hand on memory foam and remove your hand, and the imprint doesn't release.

That imprint can bounce back naturally, or the imprint kind of gets stuck and it takes a little bit longer to release. The elasticity depends on how deep that issue goes, and if an instant like that triggers other things. It may be something that you saw happen to Mom. It may be something that you as a man believe should never, ever be done, that there's a boundary that should not be crossed, and when you overstep that you've gone too far. It's a moral injury.

So, you try to remain present. What is it that is coming up for you? Then refrain from helping, directing, or judging it. If you've ever practiced any kind of mindfulness, if you've ever done any kind of meditation or prayer, even just sitting and thinking deeply, you know you simply observe what comes up, and that helps you remain present, that opens up the window for other things.

Grief ends up being like your fingerprint. It's unique and individual to each person. Not every path is going to be the same. Not every response is going to be the same. Yet there are a lot of similarities that we all kind of go through. Most people know Elisabeth Kubler Ross has the five stages[10], and that's usually the springboard of grief education in our world as we know it.

---

[9] a roughly almond-shaped mass of gray matter inside each cerebral hemisphere, involved with the experiencing of emotions. From Late Middle English via Latin from Greek amugdalē 'almond'. —from Google definition

[10] The five stages, denial, anger, bargaining, depression and acceptance are a part of the framework that makes up our learning to live with the one we lost. They are tools to help us frame and identify what we may be feeling. But they are not stops on some linear timeline in grief. —*Five Stages of Grief* by Elisabeth Kubler Ross & David Kessler, https://grief.com/the-five-stages-of-grief/

Although contemporary grief doesn't necessarily embrace that whole-heartedly, it's important know it and how it can affect people.

It has a lot to do with your own personality and your own characteristics. It depends on each individual's beliefs. For me it was normal to participate in rituals and funerals, in wakes and celebrations of life, in prayer chains and things like that, but some cultures don't believe in anything like that. For some you have an afterlife and for some when you're dead, that's it. So, it's about what makes sense to that individual and there's no right or wrong. There are healthy ways of doing it and if you have an idea that something is wrong or you have questions such as, "Is this as good as it gets?" that's usually a pretty good indicator of knowing you need help.

ARMED WITH EXPERIENCE and knowledge and compassion, I do love what I do. I'm very passionate about what I do. I feel like this is my calling. A soul sister once proposed we are the last to know what is meant for us. So when I realized *bereavement* was my calling, when the ah-ha moment came, it was like, *Why are we always the last ones to know, to get the memo? Duh! I've been doing this all of my life! I've been passionate about this all of my life!*

It has felt like a normal progression. I would love to say that my work has all been focused on other people because I want to be able to heal them, but the truth behind it is that in doing this, I have also healed my own grief. In doing this, I have also become an expert in my own grief— understanding how it works for me and being able to honor that authentically. As human beings, we all tend to do that. We all go through that phase of exploring and doing things that perhaps we've been told we're good at and we do it because we're good at it, not necessarily because we're passionate about it. But when we tap into that passion work, that passion piece, that can be the springboard, the catapult to become the advocate, to become the teacher, to become the light for the healing to happen.

I know now that I have always been called to teach, so when I'm going through a crisis, my number one go-to is research. I want to learn everything that I can possibly absorb so that I can understand it on some kind of level and be able to connect to it on some kind of level. When I don't understand it, when I'm not able to absorb it, things become a little more difficult for me. In going through Sergio's death, it was kind of intuitive for me. I recognized when people were not being supportive, and while that kind of shook me, I also knew enough and was driven enough to keep looking, to keep searching for help, to not just stay there. I could have gone easily into a very dark place. I could have been stuck there. There are certain losses and certain kinds of trauma that happen to an individual that can keep you stuck, like you're in quicksand—you can move but the more you move the more you sink into whatever despair it is that's there.

But going through Sergio's death, I knew enough, and I'll be honest, a lot of people pissed me off, and when I get angry, it's about a sense of justice and that always drives me. When I see

some kind of injustice, I'm a change agent and I'm looking for ways to make it better, and to *educate*. With education, with knowledge, people can understand it. Let's say someone you love is dying. I can tell you until I am blue in the face about the process and the steps that it takes for that individual—what's going to happen physically to that individual, what's going to happen psychologically with that individual, but unless you are open to understand or to receive that information it's going to be lost.

If you teach somebody at their level and with what makes sense to them in their language, that's what's going to be retained. And if I can just help one person with that, that one person is going to share that with somebody else. That's what I call the *butterfly effect*. And that's my mission, just to help *one person*—one person at a time because I know that with one person, eventually, we will get to the masses.

As therapists and coaches, when we don't feel comfortable talking about grief, or when we haven't processed our own grief, one of our codes of ethics is to refer out. Well, referring out can mean losing business not to mention adding to a potential client's crisis. We all want to be ethical, but at the same time, we all work with grief. So, I teach therapists and other professionals to identify what grief is, to know what the different types of grief are, and how it is that it presents. I give them the basics so they can do basic grief work and understand the normal and natural progression of grief. I give them the information so they can recognize when it's out of the norm, what to do with it, where to go to get more information if they want to dig deeper, or how they can co-facilitate with other professionals to be able to provide support for their client, as well as recognizing if they truly have to refer out if their client or patient is truly presenting a problem that might not be in their scope of expertise. It's about building confidence, building upon the skills that they already have. As therapists, before we become interned and licensed, in our master's level courses that's constantly driven into us. So, the skills are there, but sometimes the language and personal beliefs and experiences don't clearly line up, so I help clean that up a bit for them.

I work with any professional in the healing world. It can be nurses, it can be first-responders. My current course is designed for therapists because it talks about diagnosis. It talks about recognizing those signs. However, it's applicable

(Opposite) Daughter and Diane / Estelle Zaret | EZ Photography

to anybody who does any kind of therapy or any kind of support on a professional level. It could be hospice volunteers. It could be clergy.

My *why* is to educate professionals on how to recognize and how to companion those in grief, to walk side-by-side with someone who is grieving versus taking a lead role. A coach usually takes a lead role of educating a client in what to do in order to get to the goal that they want, where in therapy it's more about educating your client but also helping them process what it is that is keeping them stuck and identifying those things that are exasperating the presenting problem. In therapy I work with a lot of trauma. In therapy I do a lot of eclectic, existential work and in coaching it's more existential and digging deep without the therapy piece.

I'm the founder and owner of LiveLifeChanged.com[11] and Compassionate Connectors. Part of my mission is creating a *culture* with professionals within the therapy/mental health field, to embrace grief care empathetically and compassionately because there is so much grief illiteracy and avoidance. I want to be a proponent, to get that conversation going, to replace that illiteracy and avoidance with empathy and compassionate connections that end up nourishing people's lives and provide alignment which is authentic to their own personal well-being.

GRIEF CAN BE all kinds of things—whether it's a job transition, death, dying, or bereavement attached to chronic illness. It can be any kind of major transition or life adjustment. It can be a mental diagnosis like depression or anxiety. And with A-type personalities, driven folks, passionate human beings, there's a lot of stress related to that, and in stress there's a lot of grief. There is a kind of thinking tied to the loss of control, and *loss is grief,* right? In my therapy practice I've served couples who have been grieving infidelity and betrayal, and other adults who have experienced a traumatic or sudden loss. In short, I help people find their way through grief. I help individuals heal their matters of their heart, mind, body and soul as they mindfully grieve and discover meaningful living.

Part of what drives me are those who inspire me. These are my children and my fellow brothers and sisters in the human race, those who are grieving, who don't know where to turn, who don't know where to get the help they need,

---

[11] http://www.livelifechanged.com

who've never really been given permission to grieve or be vulnerable or to seek assistance.

With most people, you hear, "You just need to get over grief," or the myth that after a year or so you should be okay. With men, usually, we're told to *not cry*. Well, when you tell people, "Don't cry" or "Be strong," you're invalidating their feelings, and that sticks throughout their lives. It's looked upon as weakness, it's been looked upon as something shameful. And because people don't truly understand it, there's a misconception that there's a timeline to be able to go through grief.

I'm passionate about helping women who are struggling with complicated and pervasive grief, especially if there's trauma as a presenting factor. Sexual assault victims, you name it, any kind of loss, that's what I'm passionate about.

Nature also inspires me, how the circle of life can be seen in anything and everything. You go to the beach and see the water rolling in and rolling back. It's this ebb and flow, this momentum, and how when it's doing that it cleanses. It takes out but it also brings in. In nature I get inspired, I get recharged, I do a lot of self-care through nature. I love walking barefoot. It's very grounding. Grass, especially in the morning when it's dewy, or walking on the beach, are things that really kind of inspire me. Listening to other people's stories, I feel nothing but gratitude, honor, and I'm humbled when individuals choose to have their stories witnessed, when they share part of their stories, for whatever reason, whether they just need to have that release, whether they're sharing for a connection, or whether they're sharing to educate. That inspires me. That empowers me. That drives me. In that I'm part of witnessing a difference, I'm part of witnessing a change.

We (women) do need to come together to lift each other up and to inspire each other. We're in that space where women are coming together as collaborators instead of being in competition with one another, so the mindset is kind of shifting where it's more about abundance and lifting other women up as opposed to climbing over whoever you need to, to get to the top. It becomes very empowering.

It is a lot about *paying it forward*, and that inspires me, too.

About Diane Diaz

Grief Educator, Bereavement Coach & Consultant, Writer & Speaker

Find out more about Diane's offerings:

Grief Support Made Easy: A Facilitator's Guide to Mindful Grieving

The Mindful Grieving Journal

www.LIVELIFECHANGED.com

MEXICO

by Audrey Boland

"Boundaries define us. They define what is me and what is not me. A boundary shows me where I end and someone else begins, leading me to a sense of ownership. Knowing what I am to own and take responsibility for gives me freedom. Taking responsibility for my life opens up many different options."

—Henry Cloud, author

Prologue

I'M GETTING BACK into singing. There's a contest I signed up for, and that's this weekend. Throughout the week I've been going to practice. Things are looking up. San Diego is looking really nice. I've been here since June. I have pretty much always loved to sing. I think all my sisters and I did, but out of all of my sisters I have kept pursuing it. Before I moved to Mexico I always sang in churches. I would just sing a special song, nothing serious. Well, in Mexico, this one guy just out of the blue was just like, "Are you a singer?" They wanted a female singer, and I started singing with them.

The first couple of songs I sang, I was really rough. I would just get up, sing my song, and go sit down. I was so scared! But we just kept working. I just kept getting up in front of people. Even if I didn't sing, I had to be up there with them, and I would sing or pretend like I was singing and dance. It gave me more experience with the band and being in front of people.

When I lived in Mexico City, I recorded a couple of things, so that gave me a little bit of experience with a recording studio. When I moved back again to the coast where my daughter was born, I pursued the best band in town. They had a lot of corporate gigs. They sing in the hotels in the casinos. I started singing with them in their show band and that was really awesome. I was like, *I want to sing!* But I love singing, it makes me happy.

When I came back to the United States, I stopped singing. But what's happening now, there's actually a show band who I have an audition with on the fourth, and then this weekend, there's this competition. The competition is kind of cool because I met a music manager, and this is in San Diego. He says he goes to L.A. all the time. He recruits for *The*

Voice and *America's Got Talent* and shows like that. He said this weekend the contest is at a festival called the Lunar New Year. He's invited some of his friends from L.A. The winner gets $300, second place gets $150, third is $50, I think, and you get some recording time in a studio. So that's kind of cool.

I DON'T HAVE a happy childhood at all. It's just really sad. The only thing positive about it is that I'm still here. And I'm doing pretty good. I'm a (fraternal) twin. I was born in Chicago, but we grew up in Texas. We didn't end up living around our mother because between having so many children in rapid succession and, unfortunately, being married to a guy who was abusive (my father), mentally, I guess when she went down to Texas, with my grandmother there, my father's mom, the whole situation was really toxic. I guess mentally she just fell apart and she kind of succumbed to post-partum psychosis. Somehow, she moved from Texas and ended up back in Chicago.

So we lived with our father and we lived with my grandma. And our grandmother was unfortunately abusive—mentally, physically. She was like an iron hammer, and what she wanted to crush was happiness. What she wanted to crush was *me*. She was ruthless. She was not a nice woman at all. I think I realized, when I was maybe 25, that there are some grandmothers who are nice, and she was not!

I was a really timid person growing up. I hated confrontation. Family life was toxic. By the time I moved to Indiana I was about 16 and I just really needed to get out of the house. But in that time in Texas I discovered that I love music, so I started playing in the band. I wanted to play the clarinet because my oldest sister played the clarinet, but we just didn't have the money to get her clarinet fixed. So, after sitting in a band class for almost two months without an instrument I was told that if I wanted to stay in the band, I had to get my clarinet by the next day or I could play the euphonium[12] because the school gave those to students. So, of course, I decided to start playing the euphonium. Turns out I was actually kind of good at it, and I had some natural talent, so I stuck with it and I loved it. I started playing the euphonium in the sixth grade and I continued it in junior high. I had private lessons for a little bit,

---

[12] a valved brass musical instrument resembling a small tuba of tenor pitch, played mainly in military and brass bands. —Google definition

but we didn't have a lot of money, we were just kind of poor—very poor. We were on the free lunch program.

I was in Indiana and I really hated the place. I wanted to graduate early. I was just like, *Oh this is so beneath me, I am ready to move on.* What I guess I didn't realize, because I was never really treated this way, and I still didn't understand this at that point, is that I guess I'm kind of intelligent. [Laughter] I guess I never knew. I really didn't know because my grandmother said we were stupid, and our father just constantly said we were, "poor, dumb, mo-fos," but he didn't say it as kindly as that. One of the things I will never forget about my father is when we were in Texas, talking to him one time, I remember the way he was talking to me and I remember thinking, *Why does he hate us, man?*

"I didn't ask to be born," I said. I was maybe 12 or 13. I think what I meant was Why do you hate us?

And he said without missing a beat, "Well I didn't ask for four dumb mo-fos either."

I was like, Okay! Alright. That was my father. That is my father. You should quote me on that because that is exactly how I feel about him to this day.

So, I really thought I was just stupid, and I think all the restlessness I felt at that time was just a lack of being challenged. So, I managed to get back into the band—the band program there was horrible. But I'm only mentioning it because when it came time for me to graduate, I was like, I'm getting out of here. I'm going to go to school, I'm going to be an architect, and I'm going to write best-selling novels. I was accepted to Ball State University, into the architecture program. My first year was totally paid for with the FAFSA[13] and Pell Grant[14] and low-income subsidy because we were poor.

But then one day I had to go to a career fair in our school's gym. I had to interview three people. I already knew what I was doing but there wasn't an architect there. So, I interviewed a court stenographer, I interviewed some other random person, and then I was like, What the hell, and I walked up to the Marines desk. We started talking. We talked for like an hour and a half, and I was really just small-talking the guy, and he was

---

[13] The Free Application for Federal Student Aid (FAFSA) is a form completed by current and prospective college students (undergraduate and graduate) in the United States to determine their eligibility for student financial aid. —Wikipedia

[14] A Pell Grant is a subsidy the U.S. federal government provides for students who need it to pay for college. Federal Pell Grants are limited to students with financial need, who have not earned their first bachelor's degree. —Wikipedia

all about it, he was like, "No, no, no we should totally meet up after school and talk."

"I can't after school today," I said. "I've got a band concert."

That's when he knew he had me. "Wait a minute," he said. "You play an instrument?"

"Yes."

"Did you know the Marine Corps has a band?" he asked.

And just like that I was like, Whoa, wait a second. The band program in Indiana was horrible. I was really just doing it because they let me touch a little bit of my soul. It really started challenging everything now because I had said for so many years I was going to be an architect, a best-selling author, I was going to design the house I was living out of. That was my five-year plan. I was set, and then just like that, this guy was relentless.

I think he was a bad recruiter and the band was so hard to recruit for, like they always needed players, and apparently euphonium players are really hard to come by. On top of that I was a female, and I think recruiters get extra points or they're not really taught how to go after females. And I just wanted to be able to play my instrument. So that's how I ended up not being an architect and not going to college, and how I ended up in the Marine Corps for four years. What I didn't plan on was that the Marine Corps was really kind of racist, unfortunately.

Around this time, around 2006 or so, racism wasn't really being talked about. It just really started being talked about when Obama was president because of all the racist slurs and comments, and a rise of police killings of unarmed black people. So, I discovered what it was like. I was the only black female in the band, probably the only black female that many of the people had probably ever seen in their lives. And I'm not stupid. I didn't talk like I was stupid. I think just meeting me challenged a lot of people's personal opinions and biases, and they still wanted to fit me in the box.

So, I was treated like I was a bad marine even though I wasn't. It was the weirdest phenomenon. They wanted to treat me like I was an idiot. They told me I was slow. Someone actually said, "Audrey, you're not stupid. I just think you're a little slow." Isn't that wild? If you know me, if you know what I write, if you ever meet me, I don't believe "slow" is what you would think. This was when I was stationed in Albany, Georgia, and when I first got to the band, I remember trying to talk to people about how I felt I was being treated and I was told, "Oh my gosh, Audrey, you need to get over yourself. It's not all about you."

Two years later, we were in this band hall and somebody called me out. They called on me to speak and I spoke, but then they got on to me in front of everybody. They chastised me verbally. By that point I was kind of used to it, but this particular time, two years later, I overheard somebody, maybe a new marine, ask, "Why do they treat her like that?"

And somebody replied to them, "Oh, it's because she's black." I really heard it, so it wasn't in my head.

I really wanted to stay in the Marine Corps because I kind of liked it. It seemed to jive with who I was as a person. I'm kind of athletic. We got to work out during the day and I loved making music. But at the end of the day, it was such a toxic atmosphere, it gave me PTSD.

When I got out of the Marine Corps, I burned all of my things. I even forgot that I had veteran's benefits—seriously! I burned all of my gear. I have no uniforms. I didn't realize just how horribly it affected me. Somebody saw my resume afterwards and asked, "Were you actually in the Marine Corps, or did you just work as a civilian with the Marines?"

"Oh, I was totally a Marine," I said. "I'm a veteran."

"Oh, you really can't tell the way your resume is set up," they said.

So subconsciously I had to go back and revamp and open myself up to other Marines, and accept it: *Audrey, you were in the Marine Corps. You had a horrible experience, but it doesn't have to define you.*

You take that horrible experience with the Marine Corps, combined with this horrible, abusive past, and I was an emotional wreck. I was severely depressed. I started drinking. I was probably an alcoholic before I was 21. I was at the lowest of my lows. But financially, I think I was okay. I was paying my bills on time, I was building my credit, I was a good Marine. I was going to work, I was doing everything I was supposed to do, but mentally I was just falling apart.

And I didn't even know it because being raised as a poor, black American, mental health isn't talked about. You get depressed, people tell you to suck it up, tell you to be hard, that, "you just have to get over it. It is what it is. It's hard for everybody." So, I just kind of thought I was ridiculous. I really did. I thought I was just dramatic. I remember trying to express the feelings that I had with who I thought was my best friend at the time, and she just kind of rolled her eyes and said I was being like a teenager. So, I bottled those emotions. I drank. When I did go dance, I would go to gay clubs. I didn't party like most women partied. I didn't go to the club and shake my butt, I wasn't sleeping around with a bunch of guys. I was just drinking all the time because being sober was unbearable.

SOMETIMES THE PEOPLE who are against you are the people who are closest to you. While in the Marine Corps, I ended up getting into Christianity because there was a guy in the band who guided me to church. Growing up in Texas, our father put us in Baptist churches. Church and God were a way of life, even if it wasn't something you strictly adhered to. And this guy in band invited me to church three times. The first two times I was getting drunk. But the third time, I went. I think I was hungover—I think the only times I was happy at that point were when I was hungover from the night before. So, I started going to church.

For the first time in my life I actually started reading the bible. I'm kind of a passionate person, and I had already experienced so much pain, I really jumped at the idea of being able to follow a plan of what I thought guaranteed happiness, that's how it was kind of presented to me. It's kind of how people present Christianity sometimes, right? Like, "Hey, you don't know who you are supposed to be, but God does. He created you for a reason." And I was so lost because of everything that had happened in my life. It was like God had reached his little hand down from the sky and was like, "Audrey, I want *you* to be a Christian."

And I was like, "Okay! I'll do it, Daddy! I'll be a Christian! I'll give you my life." It was so easy for me to fall into that and to become so extreme because I wanted, I needed to know that I wasn't terrible. I had nobody to love me, but *God loved me.* I was still very impressionable, still very vulnerable. I kind of ended up in a cult, although they would probably not see it that way. I didn't know anything about narcissism or abusive personality types, but I did want love. I wanted just one person to be all about *me.* I really needed to know that I wasn't a piece of crap, as I had always been treated. So, when there was someone interested in me, I never thought I needed to be interested in *them.* I was like, *If they're interested in me, I'll do whatever I have to, to keep that.* I was bound to end up with abusive people.

There in Georgia, at my duty station, I was absolutely miserable. I'd been a Marine for two years. I hated it. I was never comfortable in my skin. I guess I knew that I might be slightly attractive because if I walked down the street, people might honk. If an older guy ran into me, he would be like, "Hey—how old are you?" when I was younger.

"I'm like 14," I'd say.

I don't know why, but flattery meant nothing to me, it just didn't, because I didn't find myself attractive. I just thought I was an average looking woman, and stupid. I guess I had really low self-esteem. And I didn't seem to get along with people. My sisters and I when we were younger were told that we were too white. Maybe if I had grown up in another area, maybe people would have been like, "Wow! Audrey, you're smart!" Maybe they would have pushed me to go further instead of trying to make me feel shame for who I was.

But that's not what happened, you know? I was ostracized from other black people because I was too white. So I didn't want to be seen, I didn't want to draw attention to myself. I was introduced to this older guy at this church I'd gone too and had this great moment, this amazing connection. He was talking to me *like I was a person*. And for the first time in my life, I didn't feel stupid. I didn't feel like somebody was talking down to me and was being condescending. I felt accepted. So of course, I'm going to go back to that, right?

I met my ex-husband through this church group. (I'm changing some of the names for this, so we'll call my ex "Adam.") His father was incredibly abusive. He used to beat him bare-butt with a belt buckle until he bled. Adam's mom had

Adam's dad committed to a psych ward—I didn't know that before we got married, which was messed up. I think I married him because he came to me and he said, "I really like you. I have some feelings for you."

"Oh," I said, "well, maybe you have those feelings now, but in two weeks or two months, somebody else will come by and you'll like them more." And I think what I really meant was *some white woman* because when I grew up in Texas, I was always keenly aware that I was black, and I was never going to be as beautiful as a white person. That's what I thought. There weren't black people on TV, and black women weren't beautiful. I mean, they were, but nobody was saying they were, or I didn't know that they were.

I remember this English class that we had, they were describing how pretty this woman was, but do you know what they said? They said she was beautiful because she was *white as snow*, because her skin was pearly white. That's why she was beautiful because she was just so freakin' white and I thought, *Well, I'm just not.* On top of that, I'm ostracized from black people. White people are the norms. I like black men, I find them attractive, but I guess I seem to be more attracted to white men, So here's Adam, here's this white guy, and he was pretty attractive.

"I'm kind of into you," he said.

So, I'm thinking, *Okay, maybe this is the real deal.* I'm in the Christianity thing because God is the right way, right? He's the high and mighty way, right? He's supposed to protect me. I fasted, I prayed. But you know what? I think when you have so many things go into your subconscious built into your world view by the time you're seven, your mind subconsciously finds ways to connect the dots, no matter what you do.

I didn't have the common sense, I didn't have the experience or the exposure before Adam. And he wasn't nice, he never was. We argued a lot, and I remember feeling like I didn't want to marry this guy. But I felt that God wanted me to do it. I was blindly following God. I wanted to please Him so bad I was going to marry this guy. *If this will bring me closer to You, if this is my path, then of course, I can do it.* You know? That's how I thought.

After the Marine Corps, we got married, and I was surprised by who *wasn't* at my wedding. It was really weird. There was just no support. I got pregnant soon after. Like the other women in this church group, I was completely committed to being a stay-at-home mom. I was scared to be a mom, I was just so lost. I had my first baby in Georgia, and I got pregnant with my second in

Georgia. Meanwhile Adam was horrible to me and our "friends" at church had to have seen it, but, for whatever reason, nobody said anything. I remember telling them that Adam would tackle me.

"Well, what do you mean by 'tackle'?" one asked.

"He ran across the room with all of his strength and tackled me, took me down to the bed," I said. And this started when I was pregnant. It was really hard, and it wasn't playful. He really hurt me. I was like, *What the hell?*

"When someone is pointing a finger five inches from your face—" he said to me later. I remember thinking, *But I wasn't! I was across the room!* And I remember thinking, *Maybe it felt like it was in his face?* So, I never said anything, and because I never said anything, I guess people just thought it was true. So, I think maybe people thought I deserved it.

I still don't understand, it doesn't make sense to me how nobody took me aside and in private told me, "I'm really concerned about some of the things you are telling me." But when I told them that he had tackled me before, what they said in front of him, in front of other people at this group, was that he shouldn't do it because if somebody else happened to see it from outside, they could call the cops and he might go to jail. But nobody told me that *I* should call the cops—I didn't know I *could* call the cops. I didn't know about domestic violence. I just was really naïve, and very ignorant.

We moved to Colorado, but things didn't get better. When I had my daughter, Adam said he felt like he was going to kill himself because he could no longer demand my attention. We would eat, I would try and wash the dishes, and we would have an argument about washing the dishes. He would say things like, "What, the dishes are more important them me now?" It even made taking care of the baby really hard. And I didn't know any better, I thought this was life. You're kind of like, *Maybe this is just marriage, maybe this is just normal.* I just didn't know any better, and the screaming and the physical abuse went on.

At some point I was given a book called *Boundaries*[15]. I had never heard of "boundaries" because in my own marriage, I had never been allowed to have any. I realized within the first couple of chapters that every time we had an argument, it had been directly related to our boundaries. One time when things got physical, he knew I was upset about something and he wanted to know why.

"I don't want to talk about it," I said. He wouldn't let me *not* talk about it. He started saying things, hurtful things to draw me into a conversation, to draw me into an argument. Now we're not even talking about what I'm upset about, and he's accusing me of all this crazy stuff. Suddenly, he pushed me and we ended up having this physical altercation. It was wild. I could never figure out what caused it. I never knew that it was a cycle. But for the first time in my life I was like, *Holy crap. Maybe this isn't me. Maybe this was never about me. This is wild.*

---

[15] *Boundaries: When to Say Yes, How to Say No To Take Control of Your Life,* by Henry Cloud and John Townsend (Zondervan)

I reached out and I told a woman at our new church, "Look, the last time you saw me I was really upset. This is what happened at home . . ." The first thing she said was she suspected maybe there was *abuse.* That was the first time somebody used the word *abuse* to my situation, and it was rocking my world because I still thought if I could try harder, we could have a better marriage, that we could have that godly life, that I could be happy. And then, for the first time, I realized, *Audrey, it's not you. It really is him.* And finally, I was just like, *I don't want to be here.*

What's funny is nobody told me to go. Nobody said, "Take care of your kids." I had two kids at the time, and in fact, people encouraged me to stay. People at church wanted us to work things out. And I had no one on my side. I couldn't divorce him because he hadn't cheated on me. Somebody actually said to me, "Well, you know what the Bible says, the Bible is really clear: Divorce is for *adultery.* So you can't leave, you need to reconcile." And that's what they really pushed for.

Looking back, I can't blame anybody, but I was young, we were moving to Colorado, I had two kids, and I didn't want to be a statistic—I would have been a single freaking mom—a *black mom*—with two kids! *A single freakin' black mom with two kids!* I did not want to be a statistic. But I couldn't stay.

I ended up getting pregnant before I left.

IT WAS HORRIBLE, because he would kind of force me to sleep with him, really like marital rape. I don't like to talk about that. But I got pregnant before I left. I don't think I even had the $50 to get Plan B[16], if Plan B was even available, but I think I wanted to. It was the first time in my life I wanted to abort. I did not want to have another kid with him. And I was scared. I didn't like my husband anymore. But I'm really glad that I did get pregnant because Abigail is the best. I mean, all my kids are, but I probably would have given up a long time ago if it wasn't for Abigail.

Adam was not happy with any of the kids, except Jonathan. And that's when it kind of dawned on me, *Oh, I see. You think with kids, I can't leave.* He actually said it to me: "I'm kind of happy we've never had money," he said, "because without money you can't leave." He actually said those things to my face. I remember being in the kitchen and he was like, "Audrey, can you promise me if we do separate that you won't sleep with another man?" I mean, none of this had anything to do with me, I was just an object to him. The kids were tools to keep me there. Being poor—it was all orchestrated. And (finally) I saw it.

I started having panic attacks. I started zoning out and I thought I was going crazy. *Oh my God, I can't live like this!* It was wild, just one thing after another. And I was pregnant. I went to a domestic violence shelter in Colorado. He was the classic narcissist-abuser to a tee. Adam told me, "If you try and take the kids away, I'll get them taken away from both of us. I have people who will vouch for me that you have anger issues."

The abuse had already been out in the open. Whenever anything got out of hand, got physical, he started getting super sweet again, crazy, ridiculous sweet. So we would sleep together again and right after he would go right back to being a complete jerk. When I was in the domestic violence shelter, I read about it, that it's

---

[16] Plan B One-Step works like other birth control pills to prevent pregnancy. The drug acts primarily by stopping the release of an egg from the ovary. It may prevent a sperm from fertilizing the egg. If fertilization does occur, Plan B One-Step may prevent a fertilized egg from attaching to the womb. — WebMD.com

just a cycle. It was crazy. It was madness. And you just can't believe that somebody is doing these things and they're acting like it's normal. You try to talk to people about it, nobody believes you. You're on your own and you think, *Nobody is going to believe me, man!*

We moved back to Georgia and I ended up going to another domestic violence shelter there. I called Adam at one point. I was away for four months and he made no effort to talk to the kids, but we started talking and I thought, *Wow, we're having great conversations. Maybe he really did change.* At that point I was still trying to do the Christian thing—*I really do want to try and work things out. He's listening to me. He's validating me*—he never validated me before!

But after I told the shelter office I was going to go back home, after I was there for only two months, Adam and I had a conversation on the phone and I just had to hang up. He started mocking me—"Oh, yes, like you're a different woman now, right? You're *empowered*, you're changed." He was seriously mocking me. And I hung up on him. I was shaking, I was like, *What the hell is happening?* I couldn't stay there anymore. I had quit my job! I was packing up to leave the next day! I didn't know what to think.

When we talked about it he apologized but clearly, he hadn't changed. He just got better at saying the things I was looking for. And I'm not stupid. He's not stupid either, right? I moved back with him, and he just slipped back into everything. I was pregnant with our third child and had no idea what we were going to do in just months when all of this came to a head. Money was already tight and Adam wasn't willing to work longer, and Adam was now in school himself.

I got back in school because I was a veteran, so going to school was giving us money. It was really difficult, actually. I had a lot of teachers who challenged my Christian mentality. I had confined myself to the idea that I was going to be at home, that my job was to take care of the kids, and I was focused on that. But people were catching on—"Oh, she's smart and bright," and it was challenging me. I started thinking about online businesses, I started thinking outside of the box in those classrooms. I took a psychology class, and in it they help you figure out your talents and interests, about mission statements, where you want to go in life, and I did that. I realized, *You know, the only thing I really wanted to do was write and sing, but I think I'm better at writing. Can I even do that?* So I started looking for ways to write.

INSPIRING WOMEN TODAY

Audrey in the Park | Khensani Maluleke

I started looking online and I found Elance[17]. My first job was writing a book about green living, reducing your carbon footprint, writing six chapters for just $66. That's $11 for each chapter, and each chapter 1,500 words. I knew *nothing* about green living, but that was my first client. After the second chapter he said he didn't think it was going to be a good fit. I got $22. But I just kept applying. After three months, and this is crazy, I was working so much to earn money to put my husband through school, and he decided to join a D&D[18] group! He was also always playing a lot of video games.

I started getting more gigs on Elance and after a few months Adam dropped out of school. I was staying up until like 2 a.m. in the morning writing, while he was asleep. And while I didn't really apply myself at school (I thought I was stupid, anyway), the first time someone really challenged me was actually in a class in college. The fact that people don't encourage women to go to school in church is alarming, because I'm telling you, they (college classes) will make a woman *think*. I started missing classes because I was taking on so much work, but in this one class, we were talking about ourselves, and I had to get up in front of the class.

I remember being very flustered because I was working so hard and Adam was not, so I was starting to see that we were unsustainable. We had been unsustainable almost from the get-go. We needed new tires for the car one time, and we couldn't get them. The car sat in the driveway with a flat. We were living hand-to-mouth. Our credit was maxed out, and we had no emergency savings. My father sent me $25 for turning 23—but *you cannot live that way when you have children!* And I was putting the pieces together: *This is crazy, we've got kids and we're living like children. We're not partyers, we're not in high school, we're not college students, we've got children to feed. We cannot be living like this. I need to get a job*—and he's yelling at me that I'm "focused on money!" And I'm thinking to myself, *I'm not crazy, am I? We've got kids, and we've got nothing! Literally nothing! Can you even fathom that? Nothing!*

I started seeing things more clearly and being more transparent about things. I wrote an email

---

[17] Elance was an online staffing platform based in Mountain View, California, United States, now operated by Upwork. —Wikipedia

[18] Dungeons & Dragons (abbreviated as D&D) is a fantasy tabletop role-playing game (RPG) originally designed by Gary Gygax and Dave Arneson. It was first published in 1974 by Tactical Studies Rules, Inc. (TSR). The game has been published by Wizards of the Coast (now a subsidiary of Hasbro) since 1997. —Wikipedia

to the pastor at our church and he wrote back to me that yes, what I was describing was a typical, abusive relationship. But the only guidance he provided was, "If he's unwilling to change, you might have to look at divorce." That wasn't very helpful because the entire time I was married to Adam, he always said one thing with his mouth, and another with his actions. And everybody wanted to believe his mouth, even while he was still beating me at night. So when I reached out to this pastor I was reaching out to whomever I could at that point, because one of the things about abusers is they *isolate,* they confine their victims to people who have accepted their versions of events.

I reached out to another friend and when I told her I was worried about the kids' safety, she told me she had seen Adam hit our six-month-old, but she didn't tell me! And my sister Amber, who was living with us at the time, had seen Adam jump on me, but if you grow up in an abusive home, you really don't know any better. I didn't know there was a word for it. She didn't either. But you hear the word *abuse* and for whatever reason that word is professional, it's polished, it's like it's taken out of the sexual abuse handbook. The more I started talking about things, the more I found all kinds of people had witnessed Adam be violent, and I still really don't know why nobody said anything at those times.

In our brand of Christian church, even when we were in Christian counseling, when you bring up that the man is abusive, you're told there is a biblical reference for it. You're told to "be more submissive" to your husband. When I reached out again to the pastor, I explained, "I don't know what I'm doing. Financially, things are falling apart. I need to work, and my husband is telling me I am too focused on money, that I need to focus on God first. Am I crazy?"

"Audrey," the pastor wrote back, "if things are really as bad as you say they are financially, you'd be crazy to not consider getting a job."

I was like, *Okay, we've got to stay together, and think outside the box.* If there's anything I'm good at, it's thinking outside the box. And it dawned on me, *Audrey, you're averaging like $400 and you're really only working like part-time. What if you could go to a place with some money saved up, work part-time, and in the other half of the time work on those businesses you're interested in?* And I'm thinking, *Yeah! If I did this whole multiple income thing, and each business only made $200 to $500 each here and there, that's still something, and if we can create a little passive income, we can eventually get ahead.*

And that was the idea that led to going to Mexico.

Barrel Huatulco Beach | Audrey Boland

I TALKED TO Adam about this idea. I had studied a little Spanish already. I also thought about Peru, but Adam thought Peru was kind of far, "but I don't think I'd mind the beach," he said. "The beach and some mountains, maybe." So I started researching. I subscribed to *International Living,* all trying to figure out the best place to live. I was originally looking at an area around Cancun, but it was kind of expensive to live there and they encourage Americans to stay in the tourist parts of Cancun. And there had actually been a travel advisory because Americans were being targeted, like their drinks were being spiked and people were being assaulted and robbed. So I looked into other places.

I found out about Santa María Huatulco[19] and it sounded perfect. There were mountains. There were beaches. It was located kind of in the center of the state. What a lot of locals say is that cartels have a truce with the area, that cartels will put their families there to keep them safe because Huatulco is a relatively safe place. And that's how I found Los Playas Huatulco, which is actually getting kind of big, but it's still a lovely, little tourist location. Their main bay which is called Playa Santa Cruz gets cruise ships that house thousands of people. The cruises would go through Panama on a two-week cruise and they stop at Playa Santa Cruz for like six hours, and sometimes dock there overnight.

The local economy thrives on the tourists. But the tourists are mainly Europeans. Americans are finding it now. It's really a great place. There are parts that are third-world, but there are parts where you can go to Mexico, enjoy being in a different country, and not feel like you're in a third world. It's like the best of both worlds. It's really cheap. But I thought if we went straight to the playas we'd pay more, so I found a beach called De Felipe, in an area about 45 minutes away. I talked to Adam about it, and he was okay with it. So I orchestrated the move. And we did it!

I no longer liked my husband, but we were still trying. I still believed all things are possible through God, and Adam told me that he wanted to try. I had the move to Mexico all orchestrated and by the end of July we went. I wanted to go to Mexico with $10,000 but Adam wanted to buy a car (we bought a Ford Expedition) and go around on visits before we left, and we spent a lot of our savings. We went to Virginia, we went to Albany, New York, and then we went to Georgia and left

---

[19] Santa María Huatulco is a town in the southern Mexican state of Oaxaca. It's known for sprawling pre-Hispanic ruins in nearby Parque Eco-Arqueológico Copalita, including a ceremonial center with a large stone temple and a ball court. The Bocano del Río Copalita Museum has ceramic and jade artifacts from the site. Nearby on the Pacific coast is Huatulco National Park, with beaches, coral reefs and diverse wildlife. — Google Maps

for Mexico out of Atlanta. The Expedition was hunkered down with everything we didn't sell before the move, and because we were worried about driving it in Mexico, we left the car at Adam's mother's house and from Atlanta we flew to Mexico—Adam, our three children, and pregnant me.

We got down there with less than $3,000 and I was freaking out! I had to pay the hotel $700 to stay the entire month because I didn't have any luck finding any other place that was decently priced. They were trying to charge through the roof for places with air conditioning and hot water. Once we were in Mexico City, we took out another $600 in pesos and within two days half of it was gone, in part because Adam was tipping people like $10 and $15. We were in Mexico City for a night, and then we went to Los Playas Huatulco, then to De Felipe. We took two taxis

Audrey and Kids at Beach | Audrey Boland

with all of our stuff and the kids, and Adam was tipping the drivers as much as the fares. He was spending our money as fast as possible, and we were arguing all the time.

On our second day in Mexico he said to me, "Can I tell you something?"

"What?" I asked.

"I don't want to be here. I just want to go back to America." We had just sold almost everything we had to get there.

When we got to De Felipe, I found out it was known for Playa del Amor, the "Beach of Love," and it's a nude beach. The beach is beautiful—rolling, beautiful waves and clear water you can see the fishes through—so it was an incredible place to walk along the beach and pick up the shells and whatnot, but it was kind of difficult to live there because it wasn't really kid-friendly. There are hipsters and travelers from Europe, from France, Germany, wandering people, the type with dreadlocks who make bracelets and stuff they sell on the beach and whatnot. It was so completely different from what we were used to. But it was probably the best thing for us that we were moving on, because Adam might have wanted to stay at Playa del Amor.

We were there for a month and we went on to Puerto Angel which is about 15 minutes away, but it's really third-world, there is really nothing nice in Puerto Angel. I had just gotten a nanny for four or five hours a day, but after being there for about two weeks she told us she couldn't do it anymore because the place wasn't safe, and that the kids didn't watch or listen, but I think the real issue was Adam wasn't watching the kids, and he was pretty aggressive with them, and in Mexico, that's not their culture. They *love* children.

The day after she left, Adam was really being very aggressive with the kids, and they were just being babies. I told them they couldn't go to a certain area of the house, but it wasn't really a house, it was an unfinished project that was two rooms. The bathroom was located outside, the kitchen was outside. You had to leave the house and go outside to use the bathroom, and if it was raining you would get wet. There was a house right below us. We were kind of on a cliff, so people would actually come down this hill and walk right through our kitchen to get to the house down below us. There was just no privacy.

Around the back of the house there was a lot of construction sand because they hadn't finished building or laying down the foundation. So if the kids went around the back, they could reasonably slide down the sand, several meters! So Adam and I were arguing about him not watching the kids with the danger in the back yard. We were screaming at each other. I was on the bottom of the house and he was on the top of the house. He was screaming down at me, and I was screaming up at him, pointing a finger.

And then I stopped, and I said, "I can't do this anymore."

Maybe he realized I was serious because his entire tone changed. He stopped yelling at me and came down. "Look," he said, "I'm really sorry. We can work through this."

"No," I said. "I really think we can't. I left you and you didn't see your children for three or four months. I came back. We sold everything. Now we're in Mexico, and if you're telling me that all of that was not enough for you to change, and all of a sudden you say we can work through this just because I say *I'm done,* I don't think I can believe you."

When he realized I wasn't going to try to make things work anymore, he told me, "Okay. I guess I'm just going to go back to the United States." But we had three kids and I was pregnant!

"So, what's going to happen with the kids?" I said.

The only thing he would accept was him going back to the United States without us. We didn't have enough money to bring us all back. We had $1,000 left available on my credit card, with no savings. I took $400 out and gave it to Adam and he was mad about it—He was going to leave us there in Mexico with literally nothing if he could.

The church that we were going to tried to talk to him and convince him to stay, but he wanted to go. I was going to need some kind of help *immediately,* because I was about to be there alone and I had nothing, and he was okay with that. He bought a plane ticket and three or four days before his flight, these two women said to me, "Audrey, listen. If you want us to talk to him, give us a chance. Don't come home yet, stay wherever you are, and let us talk to him."

I had exhausted all of my options. I called all of my family to see if anyone would be able to come and help with the kids. I called my sister, I called people I had served in the military with—I called anybody who might help me until I got back on my feet. I was six months pregnant at this point. In just three months I'd have a newborn. Finally, my sister Amber was going to help me, and I wouldn't have been able to survive if she hadn't.

The American women convinced him to stay just long enough for my sister to arrive. I was now *completely* out of money and it was horrible. I remember walking downtown when Adam was still there and hurrying back after a few hours because if I stayed too long Adam would lock the kids in a room and come looking for me. I had to walk down to the nearest town and use the internet café to work.

And when Amber finally got here, she was deported. I forgot to tell her you can only come to Mexico on a tourist visa for six months. When she arrived the lines to come in to the country were so long they eventually told her to get in the line for returning Mexicans and when asked she told them she would like to stay for a year, but she had no visa and they deported her. She had $580 in a bank account, so she used almost all of that to get back. I had to stay in Mexico City for the next 24 hours, and I had no money. To get back home I had to withdraw against my account.

Adam left me in a foreign country with three small children and I was pregnant. When he got back to Atlanta, he totaled our car then forged my name on the title to sell it. To survive for the next two months, I was withdrawing against my account and I was lucky I had happened to have been a veteran. I had overdraft protection up to $500. Every time I over-withdrew, I was charged $20, and that's how we survived. It was just horrible.

I started focusing on writing after that, because that was the only way we had to survive. Things didn't immediately improve, though. When Amber arrived, she put all she had into helping us that first month, and went into a deep depression, seeing how we were living, how Adam had left us there like that. I was writing through Elance, taking all the jobs I could find. When I finally took a chance and published my own story, it was because one of the clients I had really encouraged me to do it. I put off my other assignments, making several late, and took two weeks to write my first book. I felt bad about it, but really, writing that first book was what I needed. It gave me a break.

I wrote the book, and this client I had who encouraged me did the ebook formatting and everything else to help me. I had written him a book series first, before I wrote my own. He put my books on Amazon with all of the little code words. In the first two weeks, I had minimal sales, but then one day, they *skyrocketed*, and I didn't know why, but it was nice! I still get royalties off of that series. It was so wonderful. And after the release, when I started seeing how much money I was going to make in the next few months, it was *wonderful*.

I bought a garbage can, I bought a table for the kids, and we had a late Christmas. Looking back now, I think I did a really good job of keeping the kids from everything because they're pretty well-adjusted children. They're *happy,* and others tell me they see that. I couldn't really see it because I knew how much of an internal struggle was going on with me. After that money started coming in I moved into a different house and bought some furniture, and as things were starting to look up, I started to discover things in Mexico I was unaware of because I had been so focused on writing all of the time.

Epilogue

ONCE I REALIZED I had been married to a malignant narcissist, all of his actions started to make sense. I started reading up on PTSD and stopped feeling like I was crazy. I started trying to figure out how I could get help, because from what I could see the PTSD was unmanageable. It was little things. My kids would come and tap me, and it would feel like they were punching me. I used to think if I could just hold out a little more things would get better, but I decided I wasn't going to go through these things anymore.

I ended up moving to Mexico City and I was able to get free counseling from an American association that specialized in domestic violence in ex-pats. We talked over the phone several times a week at first. I think by doing that, everything I had experienced up to that point was validated. And I guess that's when I started to really hear, for the first time, things like, "You know, you're really smart." And that's when I stopped living in survival mode. I've been able to get more counseling since then, and sometimes you need it. I've had a lot of trauma. I needed a break. I needed to be able to care for myself. You really can't make good decisions when you are in survival mode—when all life is work, make money—because all you can think about is *that day*. You can't think about a month from now when you don't even know if you'll have the rent a month from now.

I moved about five and a half hours north of Mexico City, for about six months, to see if going back to the United States was worth it. While I was there, I read this book, *10X*[20], and I started

---

[20] *The 10X Rule: The Only Difference Between Success and Failure* by Grant Cardone (Wiley)

adopting some of those principles. I decided what my goals were going to be, what I was going to focus on. Working on myself always includes going to the gym because I feel healthier, I feel happier, and I look good. And if you look good, you feel better about yourself.

There were times when breathing would *hurt* but I just kept waking up. And if I had the strength for that, what else could I do? You've got a little daughter dependent on you. I remember that night when I thought about taking Plan B, and I'm really glad I didn't. She's the best, and I don't know what would have happened if she was not there. At the end of the day, I'm going to do whatever I can for my children. It's been a crazy journey. I've had a lot of adversity in my life—I still do—but my story isn't over. I have my kids, and I'm a great writer. I have great friends.

My sister Arlene, when she was pregnant, invited me to San Diego, and I thought that it was time to go back to the United States. I thought about my other sister Amber and how she dropped everything to come help me in Mexico, so I wanted to drop everything for Arlene. She told me she wanted me there the next Monday.

I didn't wait. I left on Wednesday, and I got there by Friday.

About Audrey Boland

Audrey Boland is a best-selling author and professional ghostwriter.

Reach out to her today!

Visit:

www.BOLANDGHOSTING.com

WANT MORE?

Visit

www.INSPIRINGWOMENTODAY.com

Andaman Beach - A Funstay Day | Ezhil

PHOTO CREDITS

Cover image: *fashion-photography-of-woman-hands-on-chin-with-glitter-makeup* | 3Motional Studio | Pexels

Front Matter

Frontispiece: *heraldic-dragon-silhouette-logo* | In8Finity | CanStockPhoto

Copyright opening: *woman-wearing-purple-hooded-jacket-sitting-on-rock* | Pete Johnson | Pexels

Dedication opening: *Dawn in Gatlinburg, TN* | Rodney Miles Taber

Contents opening: *plume* | Skitterphoto | Pixabay

Definition opening: *sparkler* | Free-Photos | Pixabay

Introduction

Introduction opening: *Three Generations* | Rodney Miles Taber

False Evidence Appearing Real by Denise Duncan

4: *Profile picture* | Denise Duncan
6: *Denise and Amanda* | Denise Duncan
8: *Cookware Demo* | Los Angeles Times
10: *Lights* | Denise Duncan
13: *Ferry and Fjords of Norway* | Denise Duncan
17: *Beautiful Copenhagen, Denmark!* | Denise Duncan
18: *Denise Rapids* | Kitchen Craft
20-21: *Gap of Dunloe* | Daniel Dudek - Own work, CC BY-SA 3.0, https://commons.wikimedia.org/w/index.php?curid=25465247

Good Grief by Diane Diaz

22: *Portrait of Diane Diaz* | Estelle Zaret | EZ Photography
23: *TV Show* | Estelle Zaret | EZ Photography
24-25: *Diane Beach* | Estelle Zaret | EZ Photography
27: *Diane and daughter* | Estelle Zaret | EZ Photography
30-31: *Monsters* | Estelle Zaret | EZ Photography
34: *Daughter and Diane* | Estelle Zaret | EZ Photography
38: *Diane Stairs* | Estelle Zaret | EZ Photography
39: *Beach beautiful dawn* | Pixabay (with added quote by Anne Roiphe)

Mexico by Audrey Boland

40: *Portrait of Audrey Boland* | Audrey Boland
42: *Audrey Singing* | Audrey Boland
48: *Audrey on a Plane* | Audrey Boland
50: *Audrey and Child* | Audrey Boland
54: *Audrey in the Park* | Khensani Maluleke
57: *Barrel Huatulco Beach* | Audrey Boland
59: *Audrey and Kids at Beach* | Audrey Boland
64-65: *Kids* | Audrey Boland
66-67: *Car in Mexico* | Audrey Boland

Back Matter

68-69: *Andaman Beach - A Funstay day* | Ezhil - Own work, CC BY-SA 4.0, https://en.wikipedia.org/wiki/File:Andaman_Beach_-_A_Funstay_day.jpg#filelinks

www.ingramcontent.com/pod-product-compliance
Lightning Source LLC
Chambersburg PA
CBHW051333110526
44591CB00026B/2992